CHANGE THE WORKGAME

BUILDING AND SUSTAINING A DIVERSE WORKFORCE

BY SERILDA SUMMERS-MCGEE

DEDICATION

This book is dedicated to my children. I wrote it hoping you will never have to endure the trauma of having a bad boss or a terrible work environment designed to disregard your needs. To my son: You are creative and compassionate. You are thoughtful and you are deliberate. Please don't allow professional systems to force you to assimilate-or worse-make you question your worthiness to be at the table. To my daughter: You are a mighty leader. You pursue life with passion and conviction. Never allow any workplace to steal that from you. Stay the course toward being the strong, Black woman I know you will one day become.

Your father and I love you to the moon and beyond. Everything we do is for you.

CONTENTS

INTRODUCTION

Establishing a high functioning, diverse workforce is easy to talk about, but incredibly hard to achieve. Why? Because people get in the way. Diversity encompasses underrepresented people in the areas of race, gender, ethnic group, disability, age, sexual orientation, tenure, cognitive style, personality, organizational function, education, background, and so much more. Diversity is both about how people see themselves and about how they see others. Those perceptions affect interactions between staff and ultimately the work environment of your company.

For the purposes of this book, I focus our diversity discussion primarily on race, gender, disability and age. These are the categories where most people have historically experienced discrimination; the categories people are most uncomfortable addressing; and categories where there are clear pay and access disparities.

This book is for those executives and managers who have a personal interest in or a business need to diversify their workforce. It will show corporate leaders, government agency heads, department managers, and nonprofit directors how to accomplish their goal of establishing and sustaining a diverse workforce. This book discusses the challenges I've seen as a diversity and inclusion (D&I) consultant, human resources (HR) executive, employee, and as a minority community member. This text will inform through stories and scenarios and conclude with best practices and next steps. Most of the case studies I present I have either been directly involved with or witnessed through business associates.

The recurring theme you'll see in this book is that having a diverse workforce adds value to the workplace, but the process of diversifying your workplace has challenges. I'll show you how to establish a diverse workforce throughout all levels of your organization and how to sustain your progress with fair, transparent, and inclusive policies. We'll discuss how the process of diversifying your workforce may feel like a never-ending journey, which may cause you to re-consider your entire initiative. Don't give up! In the end your return will be so worth the investment.

CHAPTER 1

WHAT DOES DIVERSITY MEAN?

DIVERSITY
AND THE WORK ENVIRONMENT

People are your company's lifeblood. Whether your company is on the cutting edge of nano-techor cleans houses, the human capital you invite into your organization to move your work forward matters tremendously. Who you hire is especially important when it comes to establishing and maintaining a diverse and equitable workplace. Building this environment isn't easy. Human beings are not simple. How we process information, synthesize data, and interpret messages vary wildly from person to person. We are also molded by the environments we live in. We communicate differently. The triggers hardwired within us have varying responses to our environments. In addition, we have world views that can be vastly dissimilar from one another. Then we must navigate gender divides, racial divides, socioeconomic divides, cultural divides, geographic divides; and the list goes on. Because there are so many variables between people, establishing an inclusive workplace is challenging. What typically happens in workplaces is that the most dominant cultural norms become the unwritten rules by which every employee must live and conform to, or suffer consequences.

Let's take a look at how company cultures based on exclusive dominant culture standards can be problematic.

DOMINANT CULTURE, DYSFUNC-TIONAL DIVERSITY

Dominant culture is the most powerful and influential culture within a society comprising many cultures. The dominant culture defines how people who live within it physically and verbally communicate, look, celebrate, grieve, and disagree. Dominant culture rules of engagement become the prototypes that all people should follow when in the presence of members of the dominant culture. In a work setting the rigid, preset dominant cultural standards are the standards to which everyone in that ecosystem must subscribe in order to remain employed.

A dominant culture-centered work environment creates variables that challenge the idea of an inclusive work environment. These cultural norms do not create an optimal work environment where all employees can thrive.

Case Study: An African American Female Executive in Japan
Kim, *Attorney/International Conglomerate*

OVERVIEW

Kim is a highly skilled African American professional who grew up in an ethnically diverse neighborhood in Los An-

geles. She has an undergraduate degree from a histori-cally Black college and a law degree from Stanford Law School. Kim studied extensively in other countries and appreciates the diversity of peoples around the world. After graduation she gained success as a mergers and acquisitions attorney. She found she had a talent for cre-ative solutions to structural challenges. As a result, she traveled around the world negotiating corporate deals, including an extended stay in Japan where she became proficient speaking the Japanese language.

THE JOB

While in Japan, following the completion of a merger, a Japanese executive approached Kim with a job offer. His company was expanding and they needed a creative and legal mind to help with the endeavor in Japan. He didn't want to place her in his current legal division. He felt being a part of that team would stifle her "American creative thinking." He wanted her to lead a segment of his marketing department. The employment terms and salary were excellent and she was elated by the oppor-tunity. Kim planned to work as hard for her new employer as she had in every other aspect of her life.

THE CHALLENGE

Throughout here career, Kim found herself being the only Black person in the companies she worked for. On arrival at her downtown Tokyo office, she became hyperaware *that she was the only non-Asian person in the building. So, when she sensed a subtle hostility from people in the Tokyo company on her first day, she thought to herself, "Game on, I'll show them why I'm here."*

HOSTILITY PREVAILS

No matter how Kim "over-performed," her team still seemed tense and unwelcoming. She had studied and experienced professional Japanese culture, so she assumed that the company's venture into new markets was of such value to them they'd be prepared to welcome her more vibrant communication style and stretch their cultural disposition. They were instead put off by her style.

After three weeks, she began experiencing a variety of microaggressions daily from her peers and subordinates. When Kim made suggestions during executive team meetings, members would continue talking as if she hadn't said anything at all. This didn't happen to anyone else on the team! The CEO would have to interrupt the conversation to repeat her suggestion in order for her peers to respond. It was a disaster. The men on her marketing team were particularly difficult. When Kim made suggestions, males would run them by her male, Asian peers to validate her ideas. The company's human resources equivalent didn't reinforce or support her leadership role. The isolation became obvious. People refused to go to lunch with her. They politely declined so con-

sistently the trend was impossible to ignore. As you can imagine, it began to drive her insane. Her champion, the CEO, was often traveling, so she rarely had access to him. She was, to a certain extent, on her own in a homogeneous, hierarchical, sexist, and hostile environment. She fought to be heard among her peers-inside and outside of the company. People stared at her. People made fun of her (she knew they did). She was absolutely miserable.

NEGATIVE RESULTS OF ISOLATION AND ALIENATION

Kim pretended to be OK, up to the day she submitted her letter of resignation ten months after she started the new job. She expressed to the CEO why she was leaving and provided some suggestions on ways to prep the company before bringing in another American executive.

Kim felt like a failure.

SUMMARY

Kim's story is real. It's an example of how an individual can be traumatized by a work experience. This experience almost derailed Kim's career. It took months of therapy to recover from what is accurately called professional post traumatic stress disorder. She became hypersensitive to microaggressions. She became acutely aware of people treating her like she didn't belong. She struggled with going back into American environments as the only Black and/or female employee. Her experience in Japan was nothing short of surviving an abusive environment. After leaving an abusive environment, it's hard for a person to be in a new environment that has slightly similar characteristics as the former workplace.

Whether in America, Germany, Great Britain, or South Africa, the same effect happens when an employee experiences a toxic work environment; it's hard to heal from trauma of any kind -including workplace induced trauma. Kim had to learn not to doubt herself. Over time, she was able to gain her confidence back and now she works for a very large corporation as a successful attorney.

Kim's experience is extreme, but not that unusual in varying degrees. Leaders of organizations tend to be decisive; once they buy into an idea or concept, they act on it. When it comes to implementing a new diversity initiative, acting swiftly can sometimes have dire consequences. The reality for this company in Japan was that women were rarely promoted to executive level positions. Seniority meant everything, so suggestions from the elder males on the executive team took precedence no matter how dull or irrelevant they were. Kim was unintentionally set up to fail. The CEO was ignorant to the prejudice, bias, and intolerance present in his company because he wasn't subjected to them. As a result, he had no plan or process in place to mitigate their impact on

Kim. This is not an inevitable reality; this situation is easily avoidable.

The next nine chapters will help all company leaders and department heads interested in launching a successful diversity initiative be victorious. This book will also help save underrepresented employees from enduring traumatic experiences like those highlighted in Kim's story.

CHAPTER 2

DO YOU REALLY WANT TO DIVERSIFY YOUR COMPANY?

The Most Important Questions to Answer

THE MOST IMPORTANT QUESTIONS TO ANSWER

I have worked with numerous companies to help them establish a more diverse workforce. They often share the challenges they encounter when trying to find diverse employees. The conversation often evolves around this comment: "I'm really struggling to find diverse employees to work for my company. We can't find them anywhere! Help!" After I acknowledge and celebrate them for wanting to diversify their workforce, I proceed to ask them a series of critical questions.

The questions are as follows:

Question 1: Why now? What's motivating you to diversify your workforce?

Question 2: Why have you not hired more underrepresented employees in your organization?

Question 3: What have you done operationally to find new, underrepresented talent?

Question 4: What skill sets are you looking for?

Question 5: Aside from hiring an underrepresented person, what talent are you trying to identify for your organization?

Question 6: In the past have you identified underrepresented talent you wanted to hire, but your offers were declined? If so, what reasons did they provide for why they would not like to work for your organization?

Question 7: How many underrepresented employees do you currently have in your organization?

Question 8: Over the past two years what percentage of your underrepresented employees left your company? What reason did they provide for their departure?

Question 9: In what ways do you feel your company will have to change to accommodate the underrepresented individuals you seek to employ?

WHAT THE ANSWERS TELL ME

I ask these questions because I want to understand what, why, and how leaders are thinking about diversity. I want to know the amount of resources (financial and human) leaders are willing to deploy to meet the demands of their diversity initiative. I want to better understand the current workplace environment and get a deeper understanding of leaders' commitment levels.

Here's what I know: People invest human and financial capital toward things they truly care about. This includes initiatives like adopting new technology or investing in new physical assets. For example, at one time ergonomics was all the rage. Companies invested millions-perhaps billions-into making the workplace physically "comfortable" for employees.

When leaders feel certain initiatives will strengthen their business and they have the financial capacity to accomplish or acquire them, they do not hesitate to make necessary investments. That's why it's critical for leaders to use questions one through nine to define what their diversity initiatives will accomplish; and, understand their workplace challenges so they can deploy the appropriate resources to meet their goals.

Some companies will also be in different phases of their diversity journey. Responses to these questions tell me how far along leaders are in their diversity initiatives and possibly how far they are willing to go. If clients have made some diversity recruitment gains and are reaching out to me for assistance, they are probably more committed to creating a more inclusive workplace in a systemic way. If clients haven't done much work on this front, they are probably not quite ready for a full reprogramming of their company. They may still be in the discovery and understanding phase of their journey. In these cases I will explore where they are currently and either help define where they would like to go and/or give them first step recommendations that will help them understand the diversity challenges facing their company.

Case Study: Luncheon for Small Business Owners
Serilda, *Consultant, Workplace Change, LLC*

OVERVIEW

I gave a talk during a luncheon for a group of small business owners who were interested in diversifying their workforces. They were looking for strategies and best practices for finding diverse talent.

THE CHALLENGE

During the discussion one of the questions I asked the group was, "Given your obvious commitment to diversifying your workforce, I want you all to reflect on why you have hired so few minorities in your companies. Really dig deep and ask yourself 'Why haven't I hired any minorities?'" I said, "Your answer to this question will help you understand your commitment level to diversity and/or your organizational shortcomings. You don't have to share what you unearth during this moment of introspection, but whatever the reason, that's where the real work begins."

AFTER THE LUNCHEON

After the luncheon a participant approached me and, somewhat embarrassed, shared what he'd uncovered. He admitted he was "lazy." He delegated the task of finding minority talent to his office manager, then never followed up. He convinced himself that diversity would just somehow happen. He shared with me that he was suc-cessful at achieving goals for himself and his company, so reflecting on my questions really exposed that he wasn't very committed to the initiative. This prompted him to take a new look at his efforts... from a fresh perspective!

SUMMARY

I share this story to illustrate that even leaders who em-brace diversity may struggle to fully commit to it. After you decide you want to pursue having a diverse work-force, reflecting on why you've never pursued this en-deavor in the past is your very next step. This can be a hard and vulnerable process, but it's very necessary to embrace your diversity initiative.

HOW YOU THINK ABOUT BRINGING DIVERSITY TO YOUR TEAM MATTERS

All the questions I ask in this chapter help me under-stand how leaders think about bringing diversity onto their teams. I find that many leaders don't think about the impact diversity will have on their organizational culture. Leaders interested in adding diversity to their workforce often don't know if they're looking for execu-tive, senior, or entry-level diversity. They don't know if they would like to have more diversity companywide or in certain departments like marketing or sales. They have no idea what they're looking for or what they're interested in. They just want to see more visible minorities inside their organization. This is a great start! But, it's only a minor part of the process.

CHAPTER 3

REVISITING CULTURE AND DIVERSITY

THE COMPANY ECOSYSTEM

There will never be a perfect ecosystem where every employee's culture is equally recognized, celebrated, and affirmed. To believe that is akin to believing there's a leprechaun with a pot of gold at the end of a rainbow. It's exciting to imagine, but naïve. There are, however, ways to create an environment where people who are different from the dominant culture are not oppressed or marginalized by forced cultural norms. Having a healthy, inclusive company culture makes diversifying much easier.

Dynamic and Inclusive

There is a way to create a culture inside your company that is dynamic, inclusive, and comprehensive. Instead of allowing your company's culture to evolve organically, you should be intentional about culture design and deliberate about what that culture should do for your workforce and business. In an ideal scenario, your workplace environment should help fuel, empower, and celebrate your employees' personalities, skills, creativity, and their differences. It should not force employees to assimilate and code-switch to adapt to dominant culture ideologies to survive. Forced assimilation makes people subtly change the way they express themselves. They bounce between different cultural and linguistic spaces and different parts of their own identities-sometimes within a single interaction-to make people around them feel more comfortable in their presence. Some examples are when employees feel they have to talk "less" urban or be "less" East Coast at work to make their colleagues feel comfortable around them.

Accepting Culture

Leaders should create a company culture that accepts people for who they are. They should transparently inform staff about the company's policies and processes, and empower them to be their best versions of themselves.

When leaders do this companies tend to thrive and survive economic challenges.

Creeping Culture

Most leaders fail at intentionally establishing a workplace culture because either they don't consider or design the culture they want from the start, or they inherit a dysfunctional company culture and don't know how to go about fixing it.

Even when exceptional leaders do a good job of establishing an inclusive and healthy workplace culture, it becomes, at times, challenging to maintain that environment as the company grows and the workforce churns. Maintaining positive cultural integrity for every employee (even leadership) is challenging because people are busy tending to the business.

Changing Your Culture

If you are trying to redirect your current company culture or build a new culture from scratch, there are ways to ensure it is inclusive. Culture can always be altered. But it takes time and patience and requires everyone to be intentionally involved. By following the next steps, you can change your company's culture; no matter how young or mature it is.

Step 1: Define Your Current Culture; Re-Image Your Future Culture

Organizational culture is defined as "behavior of humans within an organization and the meaning that people attach to those behaviors." While the concept of culture is somewhat subjective, the next series of questions will help you better identify your general workplace culture:

- How do employees act when they're on the job? Are they collaborative, communicative, in high spirits, overwhelmed, or anxious?

- Are there common behaviors-either good or bad? Do people skip work with no notice? Are they unresponsive to emails? Are they chronically late for meetings? Are they relaxed and casual?

- What does having a job at your organization mean to your employees and would they go elsewhere if they had the chance?

- Are employees showing up just to collect a paycheck?

- Are they fully committed to the mission of the company?

- How do employees treat each other (competitively, generally helpful to each other, or undermining coworker efforts)?

- Is your company hierarchical or flat?

You've asked questions, listened, observed, and learned to better understand your current company culture. Now, determine what you want your company culture to be by writing down your answers to the following questions or engaging in the following activities:

- What do you want your company or specific department's vision to be?

- What do you want your company or specific department's values to be?

- What do you want your company or specific department's norms to be (e.g. kindness personified, highly competitive in a healthy way)? Describe what those norms look like in day-to-day work.

- What do you want your company or department's communication style to be (fact based, encouraging, warm and inviting, relaxed, formal)?

- What do you want your company or department's assumptions to be (trust but verify, give the benefit of doubt, skeptical)?

- What do you want your company or specific department's habits to be?

- How do you want your workforce to engage with management (aspirational, friendly, partnership focused)?

You should go through this reimagination process with senior leaders of your organization before engaging in Step 2. They must buy into your vision of a new culture in order for your diversity initiatives to survive and thrive.

Step 2: Activate

Identify company culture habits that currently exist that must be eliminated in your new cultural design. If you have a larger, more mature company, eliminating those habits may include rearranging teams, temporarily reducing telecommuting, replacing managers, or updating performance management systems. If you have a smaller, younger team, eliminating counterproductive habits may include having more frequent meetings where you remind employees of your company's new communication approach, or openly celebrating employees for embodying the new principles in their work.

Step 3: Go for Early Wins

As you gear up to roll out your new culture and diversity initiatives, start the change process with people who have significant influence in your organization, those people exist, and you can use them to your advantage. Look for ways to redistribute resources toward "hot spots"- activities that require few resources but result in large change. For instance, if you have an evaluation season, work with your managers to help infuse your new cultural norms into all evaluations. Hold training sessions with supervisors to help them see how to incorporate cultural expectations into performance-based goals.

Step 4: Reinforce, Celebrate, Recognize, and Congratulate

Cultural shifts occur at the individual level, not as a mandate from above. If you and your managers explicitly articulate to every employee in your organization the changes you want to see and celebrate successes throughout the organization, you will have established an effective methodology for planting the seeds of change. Leadership support, buy-in, and communication of these individual successes embed new, successful behaviors throughout the organization. Again, culture change comes from within, not from above. Start small. Don't overwhelm your organization or team.

CHAPTER 4
DIVERSITY SHOCK

DROPPED IN THE MIDDLE...

Homogeneous companies trying to diversify their work-forces will not be able to sustain diversity efforts if they do not create inclusive workplaces. They will never create an inclusive workplace if they do not understand and work to change their workplace culture. A toxic workplace culture will tank a diversity initiative every time.

UNDERREPRESENTED PEOPLE WON'T JUST DROP OUT OF THE SKY

Many leaders of homogeneous companies make the flawed assumption that when they are finally interested in welcoming a more diverse workforce into their company, minority employees will flock to them. This is incorrect.

Most companies I work with are not looking for unskilled labor or interns. They want highly educated, highly skilled minority talent. They want the best the workforce has to offer. The reality is that those employees can typically work anywhere, so why should they choose to come and work for you?! What have you done to prove to them that your company is a space where they will be treated equally, free from microaggressions and hostility? What have you done to prepare your company for their successful entry? What have you done to show that you even want them as a valued part of your team? It takes time, effort, and humility to successfully recruit and ultimately retain a diverse workforce.

GEOGRAPHY HAS SOME IMPACT, TOO

Diversifying your workforce in a not-so-diverse marketplace, like the Pacific Northwest and most of the square states in the middle of the country-where highly educated people of color are a scarce resource (high-valued asset to most organizations), is not an easy feat. It's actually really hard to accomplish.

Case Study: I Can't Find Any...
Pam, *Executive Director/Nonprofit*

OVERVIEW

Pam is an executive director of a midsize nonprofit in the Pacific Northwest. After attending a diversity conference, she was hyperaware that no people of color worked on her team. She viewed her team as too homogeneous (she described it as "too White"). She made the decision to "start the process" of diversifying her workforce. She wanted to find more minorities for open positions. Initial efforts were not successful. She acknowledged she rarely received any applications from qualified candidates of color for job openings.

DILEMMA: PROSPECTING PROCESS

Pam hired a diversity consultant and they went to work. The consultant asked how she was advertising team job openings. Pam shared that she sent job announcements to an email list she created. Her list consisted of about 30 individuals, with probably two to three of those individuals being people of color. She also posted the openings on her web site and Craigslist, and she told her three-person human resources team to try to get more people of color in the applicant queue.

The consultant asked if her team attended community events or career fairs to heighten awareness within communities of color. Had Pam partnered with any local, minority-focused nonprofits for assistance getting the word out about their openings? The answers were "no."

The consultant finally focused on whether Pam knew what her organization's reputation was within communities of color. Pam felt the reputation was fine, though she had no way of validating her intuition.

REPUTATION, OUTREACH, AND ENGAGEMENT

Pam's consultant had some insight going into this project.

She knew that the organization's reputation wasn't stellar within local communities of color. She also knew the organization was not viewed as an employer of choice, and that perception impacted responses to job postings. Their outreach, community engagement, and advertising efforts were also passive, anonymous, or non-existent. The consultant observed that Pam's small staff was overworked and completely disengaged from her diversity push. Her diversity efforts were on life support.

SUMMARY

Pam had attended a few diversity workshops prior to hiring a diversity consultant. Like most dominate culture leaders, she thought the moment she reached out and told a few people she was looking for diverse applicants, the clouds would part and people of color would fall like raindrops on her doorstep. She didn't engage her hiring managers or her executive team in her diversity initiative. She placed responsibility solely on a human resources department that was understaffed, underresourced, and unequipped to lead this charge. Recruitment is a sales transaction and has complex nuances like the work of selling houses or selling pharmaceuticals. It is challenging and sophisticated work. It is work that's often undervalued and unappreciated.

The issues highlighted in the previous story are not anomalies. They are very common. Many leaders falsely subscribe to the concept of, "Now that we want people color and women in our organization, they'll choose us because we want them."

Establishing your company as an employer of choice for underrepresented groups - especially in sophisticated, highly skilled disciplines - is a hard thing to accomplish and an important part of the diversification equation. These are people who can go and work virtually anywhere in the country. So, why should they choose your company? Why should they take a chance on being in your work environment? There are companies with stellar inclusion reputations that have been actively engaged in hiring and promoting underrepresented employees for a long time. You're competing directly with those companies.

If executives want to have more underrepresented talent in their companies, wherever they're located, they will have to be aggressive with outreach by advertising in and engaging targeted communities. They must be intentional, strategic, and thoughtful about how they plan to introduce these employees into their workplace. Reputation goes a long way to support this effort, and quality community outreach and engagement can help repair or establish a company's reputation.

FLAWED ASSUMPTIONS, FLAWED APPROACH-REALITY CHECK

One of the biggest mistakes managers make when they invite a solitary minority inside their organization is holding the new minority employee responsibility for making their new workplace more inclusive and equitable! This is a really bad idea unless that person was hired to be the workplace equity representative.

I beg you, please do not use your new graphic design intern as the token minority to help you better understand diversity and inclusion. Do not use your new communications manager as your new "equity police" responsible for enforcing inclusion. Why? It's a burdensome and unfair responsibility. It puts the new employee in a bad spot on the team, and it will make them feel tokenized.

Further, it's not their job, nor their expertise. Hire someone else to do that work, either as a contractor or as a full-time employee, even if you have to create a new position.

RECRUITMENT IS SALES

Have you ever been recruited, poached, or headhunted for a position? If you have, you're one of the lucky few. Only positions deemed hard to fill, or designated for professionals who are highly accomplished and highly skilled are hunted for. When recruitment is executed well, it's the most flattering and complimentary professional experience you will ever have! The recruiter tells you how you caught their attention. They've researched you and they tell you how you stand out from the masses. They celebrate your accomplishments and tell you how you are going to make a company or a team better. They are attentive to your concerns. If your partner is reluctant to relocate, no problem. They'll spend time convincing you and your partner to relocate. They'll even help find your partner a job. You love your children's school? No worries. The recruiter will work with a realtor to find a neighborhood with a comparable school and, in some cases, will help you rent or buy a house in that neighborhood.

When recruitment is executed at a high level, even the happiest employee will consider the alternative job being pitched. When recruitment is executed poorly, even the most interested candidate can be dissuaded. Recruitment is sales. It's a refined skill set learned over time and handed down from good recruiter to good recruiter.

As a headhunter and an HR professional I can say with certainty that recruitment is often the most unappreciated, chronically disrespected segment of HR.

Many hiring managers and executives assume that anyone can go out and find talented employees (underrepresented or otherwise). Many hiring managers assume that their understaffed HR departments can go out and find talent with no additional training, staffing, funding, or direction. Untrue. It takes a special kind of person to find highly skilled, underrepresented employees. We should respect their craft.

Case Study: Recruiting Underrepresented Employees by the Numbers

OVERVIEW

Let's say you are interested in diversifying your company by 20%, in an effort to establish a workforce that mirrors the ethnic makeup of your clients. An undertaking this size (20% is significant whether your company has 20 or 2000 employees) will require a great deal of effort.

CHALLENGE

You will need recruiters trained in the art of recruitment. You'll need staff members who understand the minority community they are trying to recruit. You'll need money for networking. You'll need time to provide clear direction. If you don't have people in your company who have the disposition and skill set to lead your diversity effort, do yourself a favor and hire someone skilled at diversity recruitment. It will save you a lot of headache.

SUMMARY

Let's do the math. Let's say your company/department has 100 employees and you would like to see 20% of your entire workforce be members of underrepresented populations over the next three years. You should expect to invest the follow resources:

Your Time: You and your leadership team have to spend time building your diversity strategy (more to come on this in Chapter 5). This is an important step that cannot be avoided.

Staff: Your HR representative(s) won't be able to accomplish the staffing goal alone. You will need at least six people in your organization (one of whom should be from the leadership team) to network and recruit for this initiative. Identify employees who are good with people, believe in the initiative, and enjoy their jobs!

Money: You will need to advertise your openings where underrepresented employees spend their free time. This varies from discipline to discipline, but with Google and a little time, you can figure it out. Expect to spend at least

$200-$500 per job opening (especially if the openings are spaced out over time) on advertising.

The six employees assigned to network and recruit for you need to attend networking and recruitment events. These events cost money, but will be well worth the investment if you send the right people.

You should consult with an HR professional with a rich background in recruitment, staff retention, and culture redesign. Expect to work with that professional over the life of the initiative. Over two years this will cost at least $100K for a retained, exemplary HR professional. If you can't afford a retained HR professional, use this book to guide you through the process.

CHAPTER 5

YOU'VE DECIDED TO DIVERSIFY. NOW WHAT?

YOU'VE DECIDED TO DIVERSIFY. NOW WHAT?

Deciding to diversify your workforce is no small feat. It means you have decided to spend time, resources, and energy on not only finding underrepresented talent, but also ensuring they are treated well and have the opportunity to thrive inside your organization. Making the initial decision to recruit and retain a more diverse workforce is a really big deal, but it's not enough.

You are going to have to work very hard, as we discussed in Chapter 2 and 3, on a comprehensive plan that includes building a diversity recruitment strategy, getting organizational "buy-in," and making sure you have a culture that values inclusion. Most importantly, you cannot accomplish these goals alone. In this chapter, I'll get right into the required steps that define the "real" work of implementing your diversity strategy; the steps that will move your vision into a reality.

Step 1:   Soul Search

Step 2:   Affirm Why You're Truly Interested in Diversifying

Step 3:   Figure Out What's Not Working

Step 4:   Share Your Vision

Step 5: Research

Step 6: Recognize That Change Takes Time

Step 7: Do Things Differently

STEPS TO TAKE

Step 1: Soul Search

Ask questions to help define your motivations.

This first step involves doing some honest personal and corporate or organizational soul searching. Ask yourself and/or your key stakeholders to seriously consider a variety of questions.

Are you interested in making your company more competitive by adding variety to the makeup of your teams? Are you diversifying your workforce because you recognize that diverse teams lead to creative ideas and solutions?

Is your decision fueled by White guilt? White guilt is commonly defined as the collective guilt felt by some White people for harm resulting from racist treatment of ethnic minorities. White guilt comes into play with individuals who are, for example, familiar with unemployment and wage statistics for ethnic minorities and feel guilty for the opportunity gaps that still exist between

Whites and ethnic minorities. Are you diversifying your workforce because you are motivated to do your part to help close the gaps?

Has your supervisor mandated that you diversify your team? In some cases, managers may have no major personal interest in diversifying their workforce or team. You may not even see the business imperative behind this initiative. Are you diversifying your workforce because an owner or senior manager told you to do so?

Is your interest in charity motivating you to diversify your workforce? Are you diversifying your workforce because you feel that a particular group needs help and you're going to hire a few more to help out?

Whatever your reasons are for pursuing diversity, you must come to terms with them and devise a plan to avoid pitfalls and ensure success. Understanding the reasons why you're doing something helps you unpack what's really happening behind your actions. Honestly answering these questions about your reasons for wanting to diversify your team will proactively address derogatory motivations or misinterpretations involved in your decision, and will allow you to proactively resolve them, thereby avoiding negative outcomes. How you go about accomplishing your goal is what matters most.

Step 2: Affirm Why You're Truly Interested in Diversifying

Avoid negative outcomes.

This step involves recognizing that your reasons for moving a diversity initiative forward are fine. Don't feel like a racist or a sexist or any name you might be inclined to call yourself. The purpose of the reflective exercise in Step 1 is to allow you to take control of the ways those deep-seated motivations can manifest themselves and unintentionally harm your initiative. For example, if you're diversifying because you want a competitive edge, you may be tempted to allow only minorities to hold certain positions in your organization. That could lead to the marginalization of those employees, ultimately impeding their professional growth. You can start your diversity initiative in one particular department, but you mustn't relegate your underrepresented employees to one part of your organization (HR, for example). You have to think about embedding diversity throughout your company or department.

If White guilt is a primary motivator, you may bring highly skilled people of color into your company and unintentionally tokenize them. In doing so, you may extend opportunities to them that you wouldn't give their White equivalents. This could lead to internal conflicts and micro or macroaggressions toward the ethnic minority from their White peers. Don't jump the gun and hire an underqualified employee just to have a "body" of a different gender or color occupying that position, but who is unable to be a valuable contributor.

If an owner or manager gives you a mandate to diversify your team without enlisting your cooperation or buy-in or without a relevant plan, you might harbor resentments. These ill-conceived edicts sometimes foster situations that are the social nesting grounds for (micro or macro) aggression and conflicts. Don't allow peers and teammates to see your feelings. You've been directed, unfortunately, in an unsophisticated way to move this initiative forward. Do all you can to successfully accomplish your directive.

If you decided to diversify your workforce based on charity, the employee(s) you hire may never attain a level "equal" to their counterparts. Remember, the common purpose of charity is to give to those in need. For many, this inherently means "those who are deficient." In capitalistic environments-especially in America-being deficient is a label hard to shake. You may have good intentions, but sometimes good intentions can lead to bad outcomes. If you harbor feelings about diversity and inclusion that resemble charity-like sentiments, don't share them widely. You should keep them to yourself, so you avoid the implication that your minority hires are somehow deficient.

Once you know why you're driven to act, and address your rationale, you can vigorously work toward a reasonable plan to avoid negative outcomes.

Step 3: Figure Out What's Not Working

Figure out why you have not succeeded at diversifying your workforce.

When attempting to figure out why you have not hired any (or few) underrepresented employees to support your diversity plan, you should determine what is or is not working well at your workplace. This may require intensive meetings or multiple conversations with department heads, team leaders, or corporate stakeholders. Based on the information gathered you can chart the best courses of action and next steps.

Doesn't Fit the Culture. Are you unable to hire underrepresented employees because you or your team can't find prospects that "fit" your company culture? If you're looking for an absolute, perfect culture fit, you may need to revisit your company culture and adapt it to include "different" and "diverse." Otherwise, "corporate culture" becomes code for homogeneous. And homogeneous is inherently noninclusive.

Case Study: Ralph's Story Changed My Life
Ralph, *Executive Director/Nonprofit*

OVERVIEW

During a training about hiring members from the disabled community, one of the presenters, Ralph, a man in a wheelchair who could not use his arms or legs, asked everyone in the room these questions: "How many people in here would go out of their way to open a door for a person with a visible mobility handicap?" Everyone in the room raised their hand. He then asked, "How many people would think twice about hiring me on your team if I came to you with my handicap?" Almost no hands were raised. He said we were all liars.

THE CHALLENGE

Ralph's next words changed my life. He said, "If persons with permanent physical disabilities apply for and interview for a positions on your team, they likely have reviewed the position and duties in great detail. They are aware of their limitations, and they are sure they can do the job." Ralph emphasized that we should not presume that because he walks differently, talks differently, or has other "disabilities" that he can't do the job as well if not better than another applicant? We must look beyond physical differences, jump right to checking references, and give everyone qualified a fair shot at open positions. It's important.

SUMMARY

I share this story to highlight the need for all of us to do some reflection about why we don't have certain people on our teams. If you take a moment and really think about why you haven't had success diversifying your workforce, you'll probably see that there are a few things that you could do better or differently to move the dial. Don't beat yourself up about it, just get to work!

Old Excuses. Don't allow your natural inclination to be around people who are similar to yourself stop you from diversifying your team.

No Applicants. Are you not hiring minorities because you can't find applicants? If this is the case, ask how they would know about your openings. How are you getting your jobs in front of them?

Community Engagement. Are you engaging with "diverse" communities? If not, is it because you are uncomfortable putting yourself out there in unfamiliar environments? If you continue doing the same thing, you'll continue to get the same results! Adapt and expand your efforts.

Hiring Resources. Are you not hiring underrepresented employees because you have not allocated resources (human or financial) to recruit the talent you need on your team? Perhaps you view this initiative as more difficult than it needs to be. Write down what you think it would take operationally to diversify your team. Once you see everything in writing, you might see it's easier than you thought it would be to diversify your workforce

Don't Know Any Minorities. Are you not hiring minorities because you have few or no minority friends or colleagues? If your social and professional circles are limited, this may be the actual reason you're not finding the diverse candidates you're looking for. To address this, you should make it your personal mission to expand your network to be more inclusive. If you acknowledge that diversity is good in the workplace, then to support that initiative take personal steps to build a stronger network of diverse colleagues and pals.

There are millions of possible reasons why you have not been able to diversify your workforce. Within your reasons for why you have not been able to build or sustain a diverse workforce are your solutions.

Step 4: Share Your Vision

Share your diversity initiative broadly.

You Can't Do It Alone. You cannot create an inclusive workforce alone. Every member of your team has to embrace this new initiative. If they do not, you will have severe conflicts in your organization. This reminds me of the pay now or pay later analogy used in education debates. Invest in your people at a young age or invest in them later when they are delinquents. Either way, you will invest! Invest time and resources early in your diversity initiative or you will invest a lot of time and money later as conflicts arise.

Enlist Your Leadership Team. One of the biggest mistakes executives make is thinking they can steamroll diversity and inclusion initiatives. It's impossible for leaders to police every meeting, monitor every conversation, or observe every subtle "You're not welcome here" moment. Leaders can't control their employees on that level. Success, in this case, has to trickle down, across, and around. An initiative is not self-driven or self-sustaining. It must be championed. Communications must be supportive and issues have to be addressed and resolved consistently and expeditiously. Leaders in your company must be committed and engaged.

Pre-Work with Key Stakeholders. If leaders have conversations in advance of rolling out their diversity initiatives, they can earn workforce buy-in and they can mitigate conflict. When this pre-work does not occur, newly hired, underrepresented employees can potentially walk into a hostile work environment. The result of this lack of pre-work is most new hires will ultimately leave positions prematurely. Committed leaders and managers can effectively facilitate conversations to help unpack why they never felt the need to diversify their teams. Executive teams can plan to allow adequate time to process the new initiatives and get on board. Once on board, executives can share the plans with their teams and get their buy-in as well. With smaller, more open-minded organizations, this pre-work can be accomplished in a few weeks. However, with larger, older companies, it can take up to a year to set the groundwork for a positive diversity initiative. If you are going to diversify your workforce, invest time in the pre-work, or you will invest a great deal more into frustrating starts and stops.

Case Study: Stop the Diversity Steamroller!
Charles, *CEO/Small Tech Firm*

OVERVIEW

Charles was CEO of a small, highly successful tech company who wanted to diversify his workforce. One day he announced to the entire company, including hiring managers, that he wanted to actively recruit more diverse employees. Six months into the initiative, they hired seven new employees, which included only one male of color. Charles was perplexed by the lack of diversity in the new hires. He asked his team why they had not been able to hire more diverse talent, and they readily provided common excuses.

THE EXCUSES

Charles hired a diversity consultant to help him figure out what was impeding progress. During the first round of conversations the managers expressed thatCharles had steamrolled this initiative without consulting them. They were never on board with "his" initiative. The consultant explored a variety of issues with team members as a group. They discussed why Charles was interested in doing this work and how he saw having a diverse workforce as being a value of the company. They explored ways to establish an inclusive workplace. Leadership team members got to discuss concerns and potential risks and share their strategies. The CEO then deemed one member of the team the "diversity steward," responsible for building out the entire diversity plan. The company as a whole then implemented the plan.

SUMMARY

Leadership team members shared the company's diversity goal and strategy with their teams and allowed them to process their concerns (the pre-work), which ultimately helped them see the vision. Six months later, the company had a well-developed diversity recruitment plan, new inclusive policies and procedures, a new onboarding structure and consistently added and retained new minority hires from that point on.

Step 5: Research

Learn as much as you can in advance.

Survey Current Underrepresented Employees. To get your current workforce on board with your new diversity initiative, you will need to paint a picture of your current diversity state and build a model for your diversity initiatives that people can visualize. To do that, you need to know how many underrepresented people are on your team. You need to know what your attrition rate is for minority employees compared to majority employees. Then, you can start to establish a better understanding of why people leave your company. Your human resources department or office manager should be able to pull most of this data for you.

Do Exit Interviews and/or Survey Underrepresented Employees Who Have Left. If exit interviews haven't been conducted, you might want to have your HR team reach out to the underrepresented staff who left your company over the past two to three years and ask them a series of questions to get a feel for the environment they experienced.

It is important that you know how the underrepresented people in your organization currently feel. However, chances are they are not going to tell you the truth if you ask them directly or if you have your homogeneous HR department ask them. You need to have an external person come in and conduct anonymous surveys. If you have only a few minorities on your team, figure out who they trust in your organization and see if that person is willing to ask a few questions on your behalf. People must feel safe in order to share. If you have not earned their trust, you will not get the truth.

DEBUNKING THE QUOTAS/AFFIR-MATIVEACTION ARGUMENT

Many hiring managers and staff will assume that most of the minority employees hired during your diversity recruitment initiative are unqualified or underqualified. They are likely to say things to those underrepresented employees directly or indirectly about filling a quota or being an Affirmative Action hire. These kinds of assumptions and microaggressions must be addressed swiftly and directly.

You should also take an offensive stance. Your workforce should be made aware of the qualifications of your hire. They should be informed of how you see this new team member adding value to your company, team, or work. Your language and approach should transcend "tokenizing" terminology. You have to paint the picture that you hired this highly qualified, underrepresented employee to strengthen your team, not to check an Affirmative Action box.

Step 6: Recognize That Change Takes Time
And must be sustained.

Let's say you have a workforce of 50 and you have an opportunity to hire five or ten more employees over the next year. If you haven't completed the pre-work of helping your entire team understand your diversity push, do not go out and simply fill the majority of those openings with underrepresented employees.

You should be very strategic about your hiring process. If the structure of your organization does not allow you to do the pre-work, make your diversity hires as close to the top of your organization design as possible. That way, the underrepresented person you hire has more protection from employees and managers who may not be on board with the diversity initiative.

Case Study: College Diversity Disappointment
Multiple Employees and Organizations

OVERVIEW

A predominately White college decided to be aggressive about adding underrepresented hires (particularly ethnic minorities) to its employee ranks. The president hired an

HR consultant and requested what could be described as "mass minority hires," predominantly in entry-level openings. One position was a senior-level diversity professional. Nine minority hires were ultimately made, and, for the most part, they all worked well together.

THE WORKPLACE CHALLENGE

While the employees bonded with each other, they were also forced to rely on each other for support when they experienced hostility and resentment. For years, they were able to survive and somehow thrive. Unfortunately, the leaders who were responsible for hiring them left the university and those leaders were replaced by managers uninterested in the previous administration's diversity initiative. Each of the nine minority hires was systematically removed by force or by making the environment so uncomfortable and hostile that those employees chose to leave.

THE RESULTS

You may read this and think that my description is an exaggeration. It's not. I was one of those employees. When the pro-diversity leaders left the college and the new anti-diversity leaders took over, the transition was swift, obvious, and tragic. The division head, a highly accomplished woman of color, was the first to go. Her White peers and direct reports built a case against her based on stereotypes, gossip and alienation. She was intelli-

gent, strong, opinionated, and that intimidated many who worked with her. These, of course, are all qualities valued in other "non-minority" leaders.

Another woman of color, a resident director (RD), felt she responded appropriately to a student who overdosed on campus. The treating doctor, however, did not "like her attitude" and complained to a senior school administrator. She was stonewalled by the administration, and ultimately left the organization because - once again - of the alienation, hostility and microaggressions she experienced.

Today, there are only two administrators of color at the college. Most of the members from the original diversity hires are still close friends and will, from time to time, reconnect and talk about the good and bad times at the college, as well as swap stories about new professional challenges.

SUMMARY

What these stories show is that if leaders want diversity initiatives to endure in their organizations, they must hire leaders who are champions for those initiatives. It is also best to diversify at all strata of the organization so that when promotional opportunities present themselves, minority employees are ready to step in and carry the diversity and inclusion torch-no matter their professional discipline. Lastly, it takes more than two to three advo-

*cates to sustain a big initiative. If you want to make sys-
temic changes, you have to think about equity and diversity from a systemic mindset. Leaders should not create
a reactionary plan. Those types of plans tend to hurt the
people who find themselves caught in the middle. Take
the time and create a plan that can withstand the test of
time.*

Case Study: A Model of Success
Kia, *Department Director/Large University*

OVERVIEW

*Kia was a soft-spoken, multi-degreed, worldly, African
American department director from Detroit, Michigan.
She headed up a department at a large Midwestern university. I met her at a career fair where she offered me
an internship on the spot. The department had approxi-
mately 100 employees. On my arrival, I fully expected to
see a mostly Caucasian workforce. I did not. Instead, the
most diverse workforce I had ever seen in my life greeted
me. There were international employees, Black, Asian,
and White employees. Kia's department was a diverse
oasis at an enormous university where, in some departments, you could be challenged to find a single person of
color.*

SUSTAINABILITY

Almost 20 years later - the school as a whole lacks real diversity, but Kia's department is still a model of inclusion, diversity, and creativity! How did Kia do it? She intentionally diversified her team at all strata of her department and replenished her bench of talent constantly over her 14-year tenure at the university. When she retired, she was replaced by a highly qualified White woman who was vetted partly for her appreciation for diversity. The search committee screened candidates for their professional accomplishments as well as their ability to prove how they valued diversity and inclusion. The second person selected to lead the department was promoted from assistant director and was a woman of color. There is a way to establish and maintain a diverse workforce even within a predominately White environment.

Step 7: Do Things Differently

Now put things into action.

You've figured out why you want more diversity on your team. You've gotten your executive team on board. All stakeholders are up to speed. You've assessed your workforce and determined a placement strategy for your underrepresented employees. Now, it's time to find the talent and talk them into choosing your organization!

If you do not have recruiters as a part of your HR department, hire a recruitment firm to build an outreach and advertising strategy. Or, have that firm actually recruit for you. If you have recruiters on your team, hire someone to teach them how to recruit differently. If working with a firm, chose one that specializes in diversity recruitment. They should be able to show you how they've moved the dial on finding and hiring underrepresented professionals for other organizations. If they can't, don't hire them. Diversity recruitment ain't for everybody. It's quite specialized. At the very least, contract with an individual with deep diversity recruitment knowledge who can work with you consistently to help you achieve your diversity goals.

CHAPTER 6

MANAGEMENT STYLE AND APPROACH MATTERS

If employees are the engines of an organization, managers are the oil that keeps the motor running. They are critically important when building an inclusive company culture. Every business has an organizational culture, no matter how big or small. A company can informally develop a culture without the guiding hand of management or executive leadership, or the company can create its own culture using a system of performance standards and organizational values.

Establishing and maintaining a culture where diversity is celebrated and all employees feel valued must be a primary goal for a company's leadership team. Managers are responsible for carrying these objectives forward and consistently reinforcing the behaviors that reflect the culture the company espouses. Executive or senior leadership must then reinforce the management styles and practices they would like to see employed at their organization, which will lead to the high functioning, diverse, and inclusive culture they desire.

In this segment I will focus on the workplace and diversity challenges associated with three types of managers: working managers, political managers and underdeveloped managers. I'll share some strategies for overcoming those challenges. If you want to change the culture and productivity of your company, you have to assess your managers, identify if they have the management styles and traits discussed here, then devise a plan to help them potentially become high-functioning managers or let them go. If you do not, you'll never attain your goal of establishing a diverse and inclusive work culture.

WORKING MANAGERS

A large percentage of managers are what I call "working managers." They may supervise large or small teams and typically have heavy workloads for which they are personally responsible. Working managers usually meet once a month (or less) with their teams or individual team members to discuss goals or progress on projects. While they may have update meetings, they rarely ever connect with their teams to understand what's happening inside the organization-especially culture-focused issues. These working managers are typically too busy to pay attention to seemingly minor behavioral trends that could lead to a hostile work environment or a culture riddled with inequities and bad habits. Their style is predominantly reactionary.

Working managers have an enormous workload comprising deliverables and deadlines and they don't really know how to-or have time-to lead a team. Leading a team is difficult, but it is doubly difficult leading a team toward a new organizational culture. Working managers generally spend 40-60 hours per week on their own personal deliverables, and they sometimes struggle to overlay their management responsibilities in addition to their overwhelming workload. These managers tend to supervise by instinct. They don't have time lead their teams carefully and thoughtfully; they just want to get the job done. Therefore, whatever interpersonal communications challenges they have are exacerbated when overseeing their teams. Organizations will not have high functioning departments with this type of leadership at the helm because working managers generally are not high functioning managers. When working managers are in charge of diversity responsibilities, the results are disastrous.

Case Study: It's a Mess
David, *Vice President/Mid-Level Business Entity (MLB)*

OVERVIEW

Early in my career, I was hired as a consultant at a company (MLB) with over 10,000 employees. My task was to help one of their smaller departments (fewer than 50 employees) develop and implement a diversity recruitment strategy. My client was David, a vice president at the company. His intentions to diversify were noble, but there were more challenges than he anticipated because his managers were not up to the task.

A CULTURE OF PRODUCTION

MLB exhibited a culture of production reinforced by David, who was a great motivator and taskmaster. He also unintentionally created a team environment where managers felt they were only successful if they produced high volumes of tangible work. Managers were selected and promoted based on their ability to personally produce, produce, and produce some more.

David's desire to diversify the department collided with the company's production culture. Managers were indifferent about the idea of adding underrepresented employees to their teams. They were not against it, but they didn't want to exert too much energy toward accomplishing the goal. They were maxed out and wanted to replace vacancies on their teams quickly with the most highly qualified talent they could find in the shortest time possible.

The team's managers were promoted from within because they were expert practitioners. However, the reality was that most of David's managers could not manage people to save their lives. They didn't ask the right questions. They didn't spend enough time on important topics during staff meetings. They spent too much time on "team builders" that everyone viewed as time-wasters given the challenges they were up against. They only met as a group once every two months for 90 minutes and individually once a month for 30 minutes-those meetings were typically cancelled. It was a mess.

These working managers simply worked. Underrepresented hires bailed after a year of hypercompetitive stress. There were favorites and non-favorites at all levels and trust levels were at an all-time low, as team members grew weary of avoiding "gotcha" moments.

SUMMARY

Something had to be done to turn things around. Yet, David had no idea these challenges existed. His managers needed to spend less time producing materials and more time managing their teams. David needed to get his team in order quickly, starting with those managers. Bringing more underrepresented employees to that environment would be disastrous, given what I had heard from their current minority staff. Instead of helping this department find new, underrepresented talent, my job became to coach their managers on the art of delegation, how to lead high functioning teams, and how to build a positive work culture. After that, we successfully worked on adding minority talent to the team.

WAYS TO AVOID WORKING MAN-AGER PITFALLS:

1. Give managers permission to lighten their workloads and train them on the art of delegation. Most working managers believe their supervisors expect them to carry the same load as members of their teams while effectively managing, which should not be the case.

2. Create a manager succession plan and then train your bench of high performing employees on management best practices.

3. Coach your green (new) managers on a regular basis. They need help. If you promoted or hired them knowing they are less experienced managers, spend the time coaching them! If you inherited them, the same recommendation applies.

4. When you have management-level vacancies, seek out candidates with a strong passion for diversity, a history of successfully leading diverse teams, and, ideally, candidates who represent an underrepresented group.

POLITICAL MANAGERS

The next category of managers I affectionately call "political managers." I have considerable experience with these managers. They are mostly highly visible and externally facing, with a lot of public exposure. This group includes nonprofit executive directors, governmental agency or department heads, and, of course, elected officials. Political managers love being out and about chatting it up with constituents. Political managers can be either highly effective or highly ineffective. Let's talk about the ineffective ones. They are the ones who will drastically impact diversity initiatives.

Political managers are not necessarily producing tangible work. They do, however, keep very busy. Prolonged manager distraction, no matter the cause, can lead to an unwieldy, disconnected workforce. That's why it's critically important for political managers to have strong team advisors, leaders, and employees. An advisory council, for example, can be the trusted eyes and ears for a political manager. A bad political manager does the opposite, allowing advisors and team leaders to screw things up while they tend to public responsibilities.

Case Study: Earning Enemies

Teressa, *Government Agency Head*

OVERVIEW

Teressa was a well-respected agency head. She had a clear vision of what she wanted her agency to accomplish. Early in her tenure with the agency Teressa was distracted by a barrage of special interests requests, community needs, and peer demands. Some of this was expected, so Teressa set up a tightly knit, inner circle of advisors. She trusted them without question and almost always acted on any recommendations they brought to her.

BAD ADVICE

As it turned out, Teressa's inner circle of advisors didn't quite know how to implement her strategies and they were too afraid to tell her. Over time, her advisors began to tell her only what she wanted to hear, versus what she needed to hear to make informed decisions. This resulted in Teressa inadvertently earning more enemies than allies with her leadership team. People didn't feel heard and were left out. After a while, people stopped bringing their concerns to Teressa. They instead expressed their discontent to other elected officials, colleagues, friends, and everyone but her. Others never said anything disparaging about the agency head, but when asked to corroborate what they heard, they either agreed or did not disagree with the claims. Teressa had no idea what was happening, as she was on an island with her advisors who were equally isolated. Ultimately, she was involuntarily removed from her position.

SUMMARY

Could you imagine this leader trying to implement a diversity and inclusion initiative in this fractured and unhappy agency?! It would have been a catastrophe. This executive was distracted and uninformed. If you want to make your workforce more complex, your workplace environment has to be healthy and you as the leader must be in tune with the current state of your organization's culture and the happiness of your employees!

Case Study: Transparency and Access Lead to Success
Connie, *Government Agency Head*

OVERVIEW

Connie is an accomplished government agency head. She made the strategic decision to bring talent on her team from all walks of life so her staff aptly reflected the rich diversity of the community. Even though she experienced the typical distractions of public office, she wanted to create a cohesive work environment that was not only highly productive but also highly interactive.

HER APPROACH

Connie created a circle of advisors she treated as true advisors and not as pals. She asked them in-depth questions and set the clear expectation that they provide honest and in-depth feedback, good or bad. She shared her business case for bringing in talent from different walks of life with her direct reports and took the time to meet with a broad swath of key team members throughout her agency to bring them onboard with her vision. Connie deliberately created a culture of inclusion where diversity was celebrated. As a result, her employees embraced the decision to pursue workforce diversity and she engaged them in the process of selecting new team members from different backgrounds. Connie was transparent and accessible, so even people who initially disagreed with what she wanted to do respected and supported her decision.

SUMMARY

Connie shared her vision with her team initially and consistently reinforced that vision. The net result is that Connie currently has a diverse and high functioning workforce as a result of who she selected to manage her department, who she invited to be a part of her circle of advisors, and how she engaged and communicated with her entire agency.

The biggest pitfall of a political manager is choosing a poor circle of advisors. An advisory team can take on many configurations. It can comprise exclusively senior members of an organization or it can include representatives from different levels of different departments. Because political managers spend a great deal of time externally focused, as I've mentioned, the advisory team helps establish a direct or indirect feedback loop. That advisor feedback loop helps reduce marginalization, especially with highly diverse teams. With homogeneous teams, subtle personal slights and conflicts don't tend to spiral out of control. The reality of human interaction and psychology has shown that with diverse teams, issues involving racism, sexism, or ageism can take a turn for the worse much faster and more intensely.

If a political manager does not have systems in place to address issues swiftly and directly, things can go quickly from bad to worse. I'm not implying that there is more conflict when underrepresented employees are present in the workplace, I'm expressing that conflict is more probable when there's a distracted management structure with a heterogeneous team.

WAYS TO AVOID POLITICAL MANAGER PITFALLS:

1.   Select your inner circle based on your professional strengths and weaknesses and operational goals. Don't choose a chief of staff based solely on the fact you work well together. If you hate details, bring in a detail person. If you hate conflict, bring in someone who will tackle conflict in a healthy manner. If diversity is important to you, ensure you have a diverse advisory group.

2.   Don't hire "yes" people. Hire people who are going to push you to greatness. Once you are at a level senior enough to have an inner circle of advisors, you should be able to find people who can push you in ways that challenge you but who are not petty and deliberately contradictory.

3.   Find ways to genuinely connect with your employees. The more externally facing you are, the harder it is to accomplish this objective. Being in charge doesn't mean people will automatically trust or respect you. They just have to comply with your requests. If staff don't respect you, they're more likely to conspire against you and leave you hanging when the going gets tough. If you want employees to trust you, you must earn their trust.

4.   Be as transparent as possible. No employee expects you to know everything, but people don't like to be sur-

prised by news. If you know you're going to reorganize your department, set aside 30 minutes and break it to your team before the staff email goes out. If there's internal interest in a position and you also plan to recruit externally, inform your team before the position is posted. The same goes for a diversity initiative: Knowing why a diversity initiative is important to you, will help validate that initiative's importance to others. It's the little things that sometimes mean the most to others.

5. Share your goals with senior staff members and define their roles in accomplishing these goals. I know it seems like a no-brainer, but most managers tend to miss this extremely important step.

UNDERDEVELOPED MANAGERS

The final manager type is the underdeveloped manager. Most of us have seen this type of manager. They are the managers who receive leadership positions through nepotism, by being wonderful practitioners, or because the executive in charge needs a warm body in a leadership position quickly. Other underdeveloped managers can include those who are hired without proper reference checks or who are hired because they "look good" on paper.

Many of these managers have no idea how to lead teams

effectively. They micromanage or don't manage at all. They don't know how set an agenda and follow through on stated goals. They don't know the value of delegation and developing leadership on their team is a concept lost to them. On top of that, these executives are sometimes handed the responsibility of moving their workforce diversity initiatives forward. Yeah, right!

Case Study: Highly Educated and Horrible
Michelle, *Executive Team Leader/Large Corporation*

OVERVIEW

Michelle was an executive hired directly by the CEO of a large California corporation. Even though Michelle had very little experience managing highly skilled "all-star" teams, she was put in charge of one nonetheless. Her team members were responsible for budget issues, program development projects, and personnel development.

MANAGEMENT DRIVEN BY FEAR

Michelle's intense insecurity showed immediately. Fear of making a critical mistake caused her to micromanage all senior staff members. She demanded that all program information, budget decisions, and personnel matters be left to her exclusive approval. Decisions that her direct reports had successfully managed for years were no longer theirs to make. When Michelle disliked a decision made by a direct report, she would do nothing short of going on a vendetta to make that person's professional life more challenging. She could retaliate like nobody's business - it was her singular professional skill. She was so absolute in her methods that, in a classic sense, her employees feared retribution. Many direct reports avoided Michelle like the plague and talked very poorly about her behind her back. Those with access complained to the CEO, but he refused to fire her. He did not want to admit he made a mistake by hiring Michelle. He only took decisive action when his stable of all-star senior leaders began to systematically bail from the company.

SUMMARY

Hiring an underdeveloped manager is terrible for your company culture. It also reflects poorly on the person who hired them, and the decision can have lasting negative effects on the people who were mistreated. An underdeveloped manager can stop a diversity initiative in its tracks. Michelle was not sophisticated enough to be charged with such great responsibilities.

WAYS TO AVOID UNDERDEVEL-OPED MANAGER PITFALLS:

1. When promoting from within, make sure you have an established, required, emerging-manager training course. If you are a smaller company, send your high achieving employees to management trainings over time. Training will help bourgeoning leaders become stronger managers. A manager who is an excellent individual contributor is not always qualified to lead a team! Everyone can learn to manage and everyone can improve those skills.

2. When recruiting for a manager, be sure to ask applicants a predetermined set of questions designed to solicit whether their management philosophy is aligned with your company's current or future culture.

3. Either you or your hiring managers must conduct reference checks! This is extremely important. Speak with the recruit's most recent supervisor(s). Request references from a previous or current direct report. Ask predefined reference questions that inform you of the applicant's leadership style.

4. Conduct a six-month review of the manager's performance. A 360-degree review might be a great resource and indicator of future performance for you. Don't cross your fingers and hope your new manager will do a good job; be certain.

5.   If you identify challenges in your new manager's leadership styles, give them real, timely, and focused feedback. Create the feedback loop we discussed previously in the chapter. Then, set specific expectations within a specific timeline. Finally, provide training and coaching to help them be successful.

6.   If an underdeveloped manager on your team cannot be rehabilitated, he or she must be removed from leadership.

A manager's time should be at worst 50/50 split between managing their teams and personally producing deliverables. Ideally, the split should be 80/20, with the lion's share of the manager's time being spent connecting with their teams, earning trust, understanding and resolving the challenges team members are experiencing. This includes dedicating time for course-correcting employees who venture outside the scope of work; connecting with peers to identify synergistic opportunities; developing strategies to enhance their teams; advocating for resources; removing obstacles that impede the team's' ability to move forward; building internal camaraderie; resolving conflicts quickly; leading dynamic recruitment searches; ensuring an interesting and thorough onboarding process; and establishing and maintaining a fair team environment for all members. Managing these responsibilities well is especially important when diversifying your workforce and should always be considered an integral part of the job.

PUTTING IT ALL TOGETHER

You've explored why you've hired few or no underrepresented employees in the past. You've worked on defining or redefining your organizational culture and you started the work of changing staff behaviors to be more aligned with your new culture. You completed the soul searching exercise, shared your vision, identified management challenges on your team, and determined how to coach your managers to avoid pitfalls. You have also developed and executed a recruitment strategy complete with goals, a budget, and staff. Now what!?

There are standard approaches to conflict mediation that reduce stress and negative outcomes.

CHAPTER 7

CONFLICT: IT HAPPENS, DEAL WITH IT.

The biggest challenge managers face when trying to diversify their workforce is dealing with conflicts among diverse employees. Most managers are uncomfortable and terrible at dealing with simple, inner-office conflict. When you add race, gender, age, or sexual orientation differences into the mix, managers can become paralyzed by fear.

Case Study: All White Team; Black Employee
Peter, *Manager/Large HMO*

OVERVIEW

Peter was excited about the opportunity to diversify his team, which, for as long as he'd been with the company, had no people of color. He found a qualified African American professional and personally hired him and welcomed him to the team. After about six months, Peter's new employee came to him and shared that one of his colleagues was habitually rude, condescending, and publicly dismissive to him. The new employee had been tracking the frequency of these occurrences and finally felt he had enough proof to show Peter that he was not imagining it or being "sensitive." The employee told Peter he could see some real issues.

CONFUSED RESPONSE

Peter thanked his employee for sharing and immediately

began to panic. Peter focused on his employee's race, even though the employee didn't necessarily blame the issues on race. Peter assumed the new employee was being racially targeted. His panic made him somewhat indecisive about next steps. He second-guessed his thinking about the employee's race. He replayed the discussion he had with the employee over and over again in his mind. Was the employee insinuating racial harassment? He considered going to HR for help and possibly recommending an investigation. He never did. He considered addressing the problem head-on with the team to show the employee support and draw a line in the sand to show that mistreatment of the new guy was not acceptable. He never did. Ultimately, he called me in as an HR and diversity consultant and we talked through the situation with an open mind.

SUMMARY

I immediately recognized that Peter was overthinking the entire situation and made it much bigger than it needed to be. He should have addressed the concerns of his new employee the same way he addressed concerns brought to him by any other employee on his team. Focusing on race clouded his judgement, created fear, and made it difficult to seek information and make decisions based on that information. Peter lacked a standard, established approach to dealing with staff conflict resolution. Race only exacerbated the problem.

WAYS TO DEAL WITH CONFLICT

Conflict can happen on every team. If you have a good process for dealing with conflict, those practices will hold true on diverse teams as well as heterogeneous teams. While conflict management has many variables, here are some best practices to help further your efforts to advance harmony, diversity, and stability of your workforce or team:

1.   **Listen.** Don't apologize, interrupt, defend, or take sides. Just listen.

2.   **Inquire.** Ask if the employee is just airing thoughts or if they would like you to take action on something specific. Is your employee seeking advice, permission, a listening ear, or asking for your help? After answering this you can assess whether the conflict is a minor internal problem that might have a more emotional component or an issue requiring immediate escalation because of safety or legal ramifications. Once you have an idea of the situation, don't be afraid to ask follow up questions to better understand the person's point of view.

3.   **Inform.** Tell the employee who lodged the complaint or expressed a concern what to expect next. If the employee simply wanted someone to hear their opinions, ideas, or concerns, affirm that with them. If you plan specific actions related to the discussion, let them know

what to expect. For example, you could say, "I will investigate the matter and..." The remainder of the sentence could be a specific follow up date, setting up a meeting with co-workers, or a specific action.

4.   Follow up. Always check back with the employee, even if they were just using you as a sounding board. Don't allow too much time to elapse before checking in; no more than two weeks is recommended.

5.   Keep it simple. Don't overthink what you hear. In a minority employee versus a non-minority employee situation, don't insert race into the conflict unless the employee does. Treat every employee equally. Check your assumptions and biases at the door. If you use a consistent and transparent process, the outcomes will be consistent and transparent.

6.   Keep an open mind. If an employee expresses that gender, age, sexual orientation, race, or religion are a reason they are being treated differently, do not tense up and get defensive. Refer to step one and listen. Once you hear them out, immediately discuss the issue privately with your HR representative or legal counsel. Then determine the next best steps. Gender, age, sexual orientation, race, or religion are protected groups by the federal government and you have to take any accusations very seriously. Most minority employees do not bring up being treated differently based on these factors casually, so if an employee brings an issue to you, you must address it-usually in the form of an investigation. If there's proof that people have treated an individual differently due to one of these attributes, you must formally deal with it. If handled in a timely and responsible manner, there should be no problems. Most issues can be resolved quickly and may be chalked up to simple misunderstandings. Just like personal life issues can grow out of control, so can work issues if not immediately resolved.

I'll emphasize again that managing conflict is hard no matter the makeup of your workforce. Managers who refuse to deal with conflict shouldn't be managers. When managers are trained in conflict mediation and best practices and specifically trained to manage complaints from underrepresented employees, they will be more inclined to hire diverse employees. When there is conflict, deal with it directly and promptly. Don't allow poor conflict management skills to obstruct you from having a diverse workforce.

Case Study: Coaching Sasha
Sasha, *Newly Promoted Director/Government Agency*

OVERVIEW

Sasha was a super-bright, capable manager who was promoted to lead a ten person team as their new director.

In her previous role she was considered a very good communicator. She had a deep and rich knowledge of her discipline and an inviting energy. She received rave reviews from her peers and clients alike. Senior managers knew, however, that Sasha had never supervised a team before. She excelled as an individual contributor, so administrators thought the transition to manager should be a "walk in the park." They also provided her with management training to ensure her team was getting the leadership they deserved. Sasha's team grew quickly as new project financing increased.

NOT AS EASY AS IT SEEMED

Sasha's team continued to grow. Her department received two grants that afforded her the opportunity to hire four new employees; at the same time she was 20 weeks pregnant and planning her nine-week maternity leave. Soon, Sasha felt overwhelmed and overworked. She started to cut some corners on team communication.

While all her employees were curious about the new positions and possibly filling an interim director role, two were particularly interested in the interim director position. Nadia, a 60-year-old employee, was interested in the interim position and thought she deserved it. She pressed Sasha with questions about it at meetings, which created friction and frustration between them. Sasha dismissed

Nadia's queries as "Nadia being Nadia." She labeled Nadia a "complainer" and ignored her rising level of anxiety about the opportunity.

Fast forward two weeks. One of Sasha's staff members asked to speak with her about rumors she'd heard regarding Nadia. Nadia had apparently told people across the company that Sasha was going to give the interim position to a 30-year-old team member named Anetria. Sasha and Anetria had a close relationship. They went out to lunch together, sometimes drove into work together, usually talked multiple times during the day, texted, instant messaged, and shared inside jokes. They truly enjoyed being in each other's company.

Nadia clearly was uncomfortable with their relationship. Nadia took her complaints to the president of the company. She claimed Sasha showed favoritism to younger members on the team and wasn't fairly considering the more experienced staff. The president passed this message to the vice president, Sasha's boss, who then shared the concerns with her. Sasha was mortified and her initial reaction was a desire to lash out. Fortunately, one of her coaches, an HR and diversity consultant, talked her off the ledge immediately. They came up with a strategy for talking to Nadia about why she was upset and why she felt the need to go to the president versus Sasha or the VP. Sasha decided to try to understand why Nadia felt she was showing favoritism. She also had to clarify the *rumor directly and explained to Nadia that a strategic decision had been made not to hire or appoint an interim director. Sasha and her coach also devised a strategy to reunite the team because they were fractured from all of the chatter and rumors that were being circulated around about them.*

SUMMARY

We are all human. As a manager, however, you do not get the luxury of reacting impulsively or ignoring conflict. Because Sasha felt attacked, she was ready to attack. Nadia had a legitimate complaint. She felt like she was being treated differently because of her age. She accurately viewed Sasha's relationship with Anetria as very close and that Anetria had more access to Sasha than she did. She was in the final years of her career and felt she didn't have a lot of time left for promotional opportunities. Nadia wanted to feel valued and respected and did not want to be overlooked for the position. Out of desperation, Nadia went to the president of the company. She felt that the president was going to be impartial, as he'd been receptive to speaking with her in the past. Nadia's actions were rash but she felt she was not being heard by Sasha.

All of the women in this story are people of color. Many people go directly to race and gender when they think about diversity challenges. Age differences can also bring friction into a workplace. No matter the team makeup, having good conflict management skills and strong interpersonal communications skills will help you avoid most major team conflicts.

Although this situation got out of hand for Sasha, she was still able to use the listen, inquire, inform, follow up, and keep it simple steps to come to a working resolution.

HOW YOU MAKE A PERSON FEEL MATTERS!

PEOPLE DON'T LEAVE JOBS

The saying, "people don't leave jobs, they leave bosses" is mostly correct. As an HR practitioner, I have conducted hundreds of exit interviews. I have read every variant of the article about the "10 Reasons Why People Quit Their Jobs." I can confidently say that most people quit jobs because they feel their boss doesn't care enough about them to give them what they need.

If you have all-star employees leaving your company and taking lateral jobs-or even promotions-these employees are making statements. They feel they don't have a future at your company. People don't want to wait five years when someone else is willing to give them what they want today!

Even mediocre employees who jump ship are making a statement: Those employees don't feel appreciated either. While they might not be the highest-performing employees, being appreciated for the skills they do have feels much better than no appreciation at all. The bottom line is that when employees leave, they leave to find whatever it is they're not getting from their current relationship.

BEING A MANAGER IS LIKE BEING A PARENT

Let's be honest, being a manager is a lot like being a parent. Great bosses, like great parents, spend quality time getting to know their team members. No matter how busy they are, great bosses make time to spend with their employees and follow the employee's lead on how much they would like to share. They engage in active listening indicated by nonverbal cues like body language and facial expressions. They ask follow up questions and actually remember information about team members.

Great managers also coach and mentor their employees on a regular basis, not just when employees are underperforming, but frequently. They ask questions about the hopes and dreams of their staff. They try to shape the employee versus control and overprescribe the work. Great managers are honest and transparent with staff and really work hard at listening to their employees. They are active about sharing information and looking for promotions and job opportunities that will enhance their employee's experience with the company.

When trying to diversify your company, it is important to have strong managers in charge of those teams you are actively diversifying, especially at the early stages of the initiative. The next case study in this chapter will highlight why this is important.

WHEN PEOPLE OF COLOR LEAVE QUICKLY

When minorities leave companies shortly after being hired, they are typically blamed for their own departure. I refer to this as "blaming the victim." Unfortunately, the managers who hired minorities rarely ask me "What do we need to do differently to retain these employees." More times than not they ask me "Can you help us find employees that are a better fit for our organization?" What they are really asking is, "Can you please help us find a minority who is willing to put up with the way we treat them here?"

This is not OK, right?

The reality check here is that high minority attrition rates are an indication the company needs to make some culture shifts. If you have high levels of people quitting your company after a brief stay, the problem is probably the way you treat them. Mistreatment always leads to dissatisfaction. This dissatisfaction could center on compensation or benefits structure. It could be general lack of structure or too much structure. The workplace could be hostile. Staff could be rude, incompetent or lazy. People may lack vision. Learning or promotion opportunities could be lacking. Either way, people are not getting what they need, so they leave. That's a fact of the workplace.

If there are identifiable turnover trends, you should figure out why they exist and what you and your leadership team need to do to fix the problem. Then, circle back and use the steps in Chapter 5, "You've Decided to Diversify Your Workforce. Now What?" to help determine a strategy for resolving the problems.

I'll reiterate those steps below:

1. **Soul Search**

2. **Affirm Why You're Interested in Diversifying**

3. **Figure Out What's Not Working**

4. **Share Your Vision**

5. **Research**

6. **Recognize That Change Takes Time**

7. **Do Things Differently**

Don't blame the employee. Whatever you do, don't chalk up high attrition to being the employee's fault.

Case Study: The Big Diversity Recruitment Initiative
Sam, *Mid-Sized Company CEO/Diversity Visionary*

OVERVIEW

Sam was a bright, proactive, forward-thinking company owner. He wanted to diversify his staff and was busy working the steps listed in Chapter 5. During the culture assessment phase he became aware of an interesting trend. His workforce was younger, comprising mostly millennials. During interviews with current and past employees, most expressed that they liked their jobs, but some had left or would leave if offered more money at a different organization. Financial rewards and promotions were very important to them. The trouble was when they received more money... they wanted more money! When they didn't get more money, they left without looking back or, in some cases, without giving much notice.

THE CHALLENGE

Sam was frustrated. He sat down with an HR and diversity consultant and looked at his options. The types of jobs he offered attracted a lot of millennials who valued financial reward as the most important way to celebrate their contributions to the team. They wanted promotions, too. The idea of working up to a promotion after ten to 20 years of loyal service at the same job was not their idea of a good time. The fact is, younger employees are more mobile, have fewer attachments and loyalties, and many are highly skilled and in high demand.

THE SOLUTION

The consultant suggested that instead of fighting against the millennials' generational tendencies, why not build HR systems that recognized Sam's target workforce's tendencies. This falls outside the realm of stereotyping because lots of studies have been done on modern workplace trends. Younger workers do have different expectations. So, is it possible to build an organizational structure, compensation and benefits plan, and company policies and practices targeted toward that group? The new structure will also naturally support and benefit all employees. Who doesn't want more money and more promotional opportunities more quickly? The new structure will force managers out of their comfort zones and to be more creative. Management isn't about the managers; it's about the teams they lead. How we make employees feel on our team or in our companies matters-a lot!

Case Study: Chip on the Shoulder Cliché
Karla, *Director Of Communications/Large Private Organization*

OVERVIEW

Karla was an accomplished and confident Latina woman who was director of communications for a large organization. She was highly educated and came with an impressive list of accomplishments and references. The organization appeared to be committed to finding and hiring highly educated diverse talent. The recruiters were some of the best at creating the appearance that their organization was the "best" place to work and thrive.

THE CHALLENGE

Karla immediately noticed a trend. Most of the minority hires would leave the company after 12 to 18 months. Over time the non-minority employees would openly say disparaging things about the minority employees that left.

Karla sometimes pushed against the status quo by asking really smart questions that forced people to have hard discussions. It became clear that some did not like Karla's ability to challenge the company's ways of engaging with community members and stakeholders. They also didn't like the fact that she was constantly asking them to help her understand the contradiction between what they said they were going to do and what they actually did. They started icing Karla out. She wasn't invited to strategy meetings. She was conveniently left off all director invitations.

After a few months of enduring this terrible behavior, Karla left the organization without apology. She had a wonderful wealth of knowledge and expertise. She would not tolerate the alienation and resentment she experi-

enced.

THE AFTERMATH

Some of Karla's peers said despicable things about her after she left. Because she was opinionated, she was labeled "hard to work with." They claimed she was not "as good of a communications person" as they thought. She was branded as aggressive and hostile, oblivious to knowing the appropriate time and place to ask questions. All the fingers of blame were pointed directly at Karla.

SUMMARY

Karla was and is still amazing. While the reputation attacks made it hard for Karla to find another job, she eventually did. She also sued the company and won.

Blaming minority employees who leave your organization for being the problem is immature and reckless. Take ownership and move on. You will not like every employee you hire, but you do not have the right to sully their reputation when they leave your company.

CHAPTER 8

ADDITIONAL PITFALLS OF DIVERSIFICATION

Addressing Tokenism, Affirmative Action, Community Connections, and Inclusion

The recurring theme in this book is that r
versity initiative is challenging work. Wh
the driver of this process or you delega'
move the initiative forward, it's a proc
obstacles. In my line of work I meet with manage
larly about their new or current diversity initiatives and
they share their challenges with me. The most common
are as follows:

1. Tokenizing the work.

2. Seeing Affirmative Action compliance and diver-
    sity and inclusion as interchangeable efforts.

3. Adopting a "by any means" hiring motto.

THE LANGUAGE OF EXCLUSION

The real challenge of inclusion is breaking the code of
exclusion. Language and words have power. They can
either bridge differences or widen the gap. So, let's dive
into this with our eyes open. Exclusion comes with its
own set of ciphers. The first is tokenism.

Merriam-Webster Dictionary defines tokenism as the
practice of making only a perfunctory or symbolic effort
to do a particular thing, especially by recruiting a small
number of people from underrepresented groups in order to give the appearance of sexual or racial equality

thin a workforce. Beautiful. I couldn't have said it better if you paid me! Some executives only want to give the appearance of being passionate about diversity and inclusion. Tokenizing the work of recruiting a diverse workforce, the diversity initiative itself, or the people brought in as a result of the initiative, can be incredibly harmful to the employees you bring into your company and your company as a whole. It can lead to high attrition and a poor company reputation. It's easier and more cost-effective to do it "right."

If you have to ask, "Am I tokenizing the work," here are a few ways you can determine whether you are engaging in the practice:

- You believe you only have to hire one or two minorities to accomplish your diversity initiative. This is not true. Diversity and inclusion is a system-wide initiative; hiring one or two people is a great start, but if your focus is simply checking the "mission accomplished" box after hiring two people, you, my friend, are indulging in tokenism.

- You hire a diversity and inclusion consultant or employee expecting them to be solely responsible for the "equity work" for your company. In fact, equity must be everyone's responsibility. To place all of your diversity and inclusion (D&I) work on one person or team, no matter the size of your company, is tokenism. It also places the person or persons in charge of the D&I work in a tough spot. Employees in your company will view them as the equity police. Managers will often avoid working with them on projects that are not explicitly diversity centered. People also may not see the relevance of having a D&I representative at a budget, marketing, or operations discussion, which really restricts their scope of equity work. You talk about or think about equity only when it's time to give a public presentation or speech to stakeholder groups who care care about equity. If you are not engaging in discussions about D&I on a regularly scheduled basis, you've probably tokenized the initiative.

DIVERSITY AND INCLUSION IS NOT AFFIRMATIVE ACTION

Affirmative Action and D&I are two unique disciplines that are often confused for being the same thing. Affirmative Action spawned from the Civil Rights movement and equal employment opportunity legislation of the 60's and is rooted in legal compliance. Employers are expected to make a positive effort to recruit, hire, train, and promote employees of legally defined minority groups. D&I, on the other hand, is strategically driven and brings pragmatism to diversity work. It focuses on benefits to the organization. D&I is generally viewed as a positive contributor to organizational goals such as profit, productivity, and moral. It encompasses much more than just avoiding lawsuits and meeting legal requirements.

Affirmative Action generally uses an assimilation approach that of expecting people brought into the system to adapt to existing conditions. D&I operates from a different approach, a more synergistic model. This view assumes that the diverse groups will devise new, creative ways of working that will move beyond the way companies have done business as usual.

Finally, Affirmative Action is numbers-oriented and aimed at changing the demographics within an organization. D&I is more behavior-oriented, aimed at changing the organizational culture, and developing skills and policies that get the best from everyone. To put it bluntly, Affirmative Action opens doors. That's still important. D&I opens the culture and the system. Managing diversity does not replace Affirmative Action; rather, it builds on the critical foundation laid by workplace equity programs.

Affirmative Action and managing diversity initiatives go hand-in-hand; each reinforces the gains of the other. Without the affirmative commitment to hire and promote diverse employees, organizations would rarely be motivated to expand beyond their comfort zone to include those who are different. Once diverse employees are on board, the organization can focus on creating an environment inclusive of everyone's needs and values. Affirmative Action will not necessarily lead to an inclusive work environment. Affirmative Action can facilitate bringing people into your workplace, but D&I policies will keep people engaged and happy in your workplace.

ARE WE TIRED OF STEREOTYPES YET?

Hiring "by any means" refers to hiring in a hurry because you want to get someone into your organization fast. This means hiring candidates who are underqualified, a bad fit for the job, terrible leaders, ineffective managers, or dispassionate team leaders. This is a bad hiring strategy in general, and it damages more when it comes to hiring underrepresented candidates.

Underrepresented candidates, particularly ethnic minorities, have stereotypes that they have to face every day of their lives. It's not a chip on their shoulder or an attitude. It's a reality. When you hire an employee from an underrepresented group "by any means" and they are unprepared to be successful in the job, you possibly set them up to confirm negative stereotypes about their minority group.

For instance, when I Google racial and gender stereo-types, the following things pop up:

Blacks:

Black people are angry, intellectually inferior, and lazy.

Latinos:

Don't speak English well. Have lots of children. Work exclusively in agriculture and housekeeping.

Muslims:

Rigid and sexist.

Sex:

Women are emotional, less strategic, and bitchy.

Case Study: Unqualified Female Construction Worker

Joe, *CEO/Large Construction Firm*

OVERVIEW

Joe owned a large construction company. He considered himself fair, liberal, inclusive, and unbiased. One day after a planning meeting on a new, large project he looked around the room and noticed there were only White men at the table. He approached the general manager after the meeting and asked, "Am I doing something wrong? Are there no women qualified to manage any of my proj-

ects?" The GM shrugged his shoulders and said, "I don't know. Ain't no women ever asked about it." From that point on, Joe made up his mind to find a "woman director," come hell or high water.

Joe advertised a management position and actively looked for resumes from women. All the female applicants were unqualified, but Joe closed his eyes and picked the first one his finger landed on, literally. Even though he knew she wasn't the best candidate for the job, he hired her anyway and put her to work.

THE CHALLENGE

Within the first three months people started complaining about the new hire. She didn't seem to know the ins and outs of the job well enough to direct and lead her all male team. Jokes circulated about "What she had to do to get the job." At staff meetings, she was cut out of discussions. Her team generally made her life unbearable. Eventually, Joe had to admit his error and fire her.

SUMMARY

Hiring people under a diversity umbrella means you have to be very diligent in determining the skill level of the people you bring in. Hiring underrepresented employees that are underqualified for positions will derail your diversity initiative and cause your workforce to question your leadership. Don't do it. If you and your team do the work of broad advertising and vetting candidates, aces aren't hard to find! You just have to know where to look in the deck.

CONNECTING IMPORTS TO THE COMMUNITY

Many companies in less-diverse parts of the country import their minority talent to the region. When this recruitment strategy is employed, attrition is normally high for the underrepresented hires within the first three years of their time with the organization. As an executive recruiter, I have imported my fair share of minority talent to companies. One thing I strongly advise my clients to do once the employee is hired is connect them to their local community.

In less-diverse regions, such as the Pacific Northwest, imported minority employees, in particular, need to find a place in their new city or region. You cannot assume you know what they need to feel at home. If your employee is a non-native English speaker, having space to speak their native language is probably very important to them. If they are people of color, social opportunities with other people of color will be very important to them. All cultures are unique, and minorities engage with minority communities in varied and complex ways.

The reality is that culture matters outside of the work-place, too.

Don't set up your new hires for failure. Make that ex-tra effort to connect with your local Hispanic chamber, NAACP, Urban League, Asian/Pacific Islander commu-nity groups, LGBTQ groups, and others. Figure out ways your new hires can connect with those organizations. They will be able to connect them to the city's profes-sional and social minority communities quickly.

How should you go about this? Call the organizations and schedule time to meet with a representative one-on-one and ask what kinds of networking/social events they have and how you can get your new employees in-volved. Create a catalog of resources and invite all new hires to get involved. You can do this for a variety of ex-ternal resources, including LGBTQ, racial, religious, and local cultural events. All new hires will appreciate this kind of effort; minority employees will especially appre-ciate it. As you move toward acknowledging the value of underrepresented cultures, you'll also understand why minorities value their community connections so much.

Case Study: Two- to Three-Year Itch
Tech Firm

OVERVIEW

A Northwest technology firm was desperate to identify ways to retain their talent of color. The company's executive team ran the numbers and saw they were spending a great deal of time and money recruiting minority talent only to lose them within two to three years.

RESEARCH

After reviewing exit interview statements, the firm identified that people were leaving because they did not like the region. They felt disconnected, isolated, and struggled socially. The company hired a diversity consultant to work with their company's employee resource group (ERG).

THE PLAN

The consultant's first step was to help the company's ERG connect with ERGs at other Northwest companies. The consultant helped them connect with Black, Asian, Latino, and LGBTQ groups at other tech companies. The connections helped new hires expand their social networks quickly.

ERGs can positively impact companies and their workforces if used properly. They also help reinforce the value of workforce diversity and community connections.

CHAPTER 9

THE TRUTH ABOUT HR

*They Can Hurt
or Help the Process*

I have a theory: If HR and D&I professionals united, workplace equity could be realized overnight. Why? Because in most work environments, D&I and HR professionals avoid each other like the plague. I have worked in both camps and gone to conferences with both sets of professionals, so I know how they relate to one another. They constantly complain about each other. Many senior D&I professionals have some of the following negative opinions about HR professionals.

NEGATIVE VIEWS OF HR PROFESSIONALS FROM D&I PROFESSIONALS

1. HR doesn't fulfill its core function, which is to ensure that all employees feel welcomed versus some feeling like outsiders. Diversity and inclusion practitioners know that some employees feel marginalized because those people go to D&I for support.

2. HR is often too homogeneous. Most HR departments in America are predominantly composed of White women. HR is supposed to be the place where people can come and feel safe expressing how they feel at work. People feel less safe, less understood, and less comfortable going to HR

with their concerns because HR is so dominant-culture oriented.

3. HR is too rigid and too stuck in the past. HR has become the second most disliked departments in American companies, second only to IT departments (Totally my opinion). Human resources tends to be the department of "No." They tend to be transaction-minded and don't think about human capital solutions and business opportunities unless prompted. Human resource staff members tend to have less formal education around their craft and are less creative and proactive about how they approach their work. They usually learn their craft on the job in homogeneous environments, and they can be closed-minded about social and cultural shifts that could be instrumental in creating an inclusive workplace.

4. Human resources doesn't treat issues equitably, therefore they don't treat people equitably. Many D&I practitioners hear from underrepresented employees after they've gone to HR with a concern and don't feel like they were heard. This is a very one-sided criticism, but it has some truth to it. When an underrepresented employee gathers enough courage to go to HR with a concern and HR tries to talk them down and/or minimizes their truth, those employees tend to feel like HR

is a part of the exclusionary problem. They often feel victimized again by their experience with HR and afterward they usually harbor ill feelings for HR. If the company has a D&I department, those employees will typically go to them and ask for guidance and encouragement.

5. Human resources writes policies without people from different walks of life in mind, or HR doesn't enforce policies that disproportionately impact historically underserved and underrepresented employees. To showcase this stereotype held by many D&I practitioners, let's talk about money. HR departments know what's happening on all compensation and benefits fronts. HR has the responsibility to ensure pay equity is established and maintained, and yet HR departments allow hiring managers to systematically pay women and minorities less than their White, male counterparts every day! HR is also responsible for building up a company's workforce. They know the company's Affirmative Action goals and/or workforce diversity initiatives. They know the hiring policies and practices that exist and where there are holes in each. They know which managers don't adhere to hiring policies and where there is practice creep. They should be updating antiquated policies and practices and adopting new ones; they should be

training and coaching managers and executives on the value of these policies; and they should consistently remind employees of the company›s larger goals. Do most HR departments operate in this way? No. This is why D&I practitioners tend to really struggle with HR!

Human resources is not solely to blame for diversity initiative shortcomings. Leadership is more often to blame. When companies won't allow HR to have a voice at the executive table, they are forcing HR to remain transactional and reactive. When HR is buried in the finance division, the creative possibilities of HR are stifled. When HR is severely understaffed and underpaid, leadership is guaranteeing that HR will remain one-dimensional and exclusively transactional.

If you are a smaller business without an HR representative on your team and are planning to expand, I recommend that you immediately hire or contract with a part-time HR professional. Hire one that's great at creative HR designs and solutions. Is this hard to find? Yes, but it's necessary. Make your HR representative an integral part of your executive team. The impact will be resounding and this decision will also positively impact your bottom line.

Case Study: HR Success
Serilda, *Human Resources Director*

OVERVIEW

Many years ago, I accepted the position of first human resources director (HRD) of color to serve on a large, established, company's executive team. I was responsible for helping to shift the company culture. Minority employees expressed that the company culture was hostile toward them and management wanted me to address this and recruit more people of color for the company. They also hoped that ultimately their workforce would more accurately reflect their consumer base. Super cool job, I know!

THE CHALLENGE

My team was predominantly White women, all of whom were significantly older than I was. This team was almost exclusively transactional. Their reputation was that they made excuses any time the executive team requested anything from them. The chief of staff told me to be prepared to "clean house" if I had to and start from scratch. I heard her words, but wanted to evaluate the situation independently and form my own conclusions.

CAREFUL EVALUATION

My style of leadership was very different from what the team was used to. I assessed them for months to identify their strengths and weaknesses. They were timid, shy,

and very accommodating; they never questioned anything I had to say and never pushed back. In many ways
they engaged with me the way an abused child would.

I FREAKIN' HATED IT!

*I personally believe the best teams on the planet are ones
where staff members ask questions, challenge assumptions, respectfully critique, and offer alternative solutions! I wanted to hear their opinions. I wanted to hear
their suggestions. They hadn't ever been led the way I
was leading them. They were also accustomed to being
told what to do, and not asked for their opinions on solutions. In addition, they weren't used to their leader having
a voice at the table where strategic decisions were made.
They didn't know how to react to the new positioning of
their department. They'd also been told subtly and not-
so-subtly by the executive team that they were incompetent, which was demoralizing.*

*Over time I earned the team's trust and helped them see
that it was ok to disagree with me. I also pushed against
passive recruitment practices, lack of proactive client
engagement, and waiting for a complaint or a request to
make a change they already knew was needed. I helped
them see the value of treating the company's workforce
as clients instead of customers (think fast food's "May I
take your order," versus legal advice from an attorney at
a law firm).*

SUMMARY

*Within six months we asked to participate in managers'
staff meetings and proactively asked staff how we could
support them in different ways. We asked them questions in ways that made them look at us differently and
launched a marketing initiative to help people see the
different ways they could engage with us. The campaign
had web-based and print elements and we visited every
single team in the company to tell them we wanted to
help make their professional dreams come true. We invited them to come and speak with us about any and everything.*

*Word spread through the company like wildfire. "HR is
the truth. They actually help!" Managers, represented
staff, and underrepresented staff alike were reaching
out all the time. They reached out to the employee relations people, recruiters, and learning and organizational
development folks. Everyone. For the first time ever, minority employees began stopping by and telling us about
their experiences. At first they only wanted to meet with
me, but I introduced them to members of my team and
those members listened, offered advice, and followed
through with investigations or resources. I pushed back
at the executive level about business suggestions rooted
in past practices that we knew would continue to margin-
alize certain groups of people. These outdated practices
wouldn't help move the dial toward the cultural shifts the*

company wanted to see.

Not everyone was happy with the outcome, but they re-spected my team and me for being consistent, creative, and engaged. Within two years I'd radically elevated the profile of HR. Managers and teams loved us! We earned the trust of the company and we helped shift the culture while doing so!

I believe culture is created and reinforced within HR. We know when environments are harming people. We know when there are unfair and biased hiring and promotional practices at play. We know when and where there is ma-jor conflict happening and we know when there are toxic leaders in departments. We need to combat behaviors that are antithetical to the culture the company desires. We need to reinforce and train staff and managers to support the behaviors we know will foster the work cul-ture we want. By doing so we can eliminate exclusionary practices and homogeneity that leads to the marginal-ization of entire groups of employees.

NEGATIVE VIEWS OF DIVERSITY AND INCLUSION PROFESSIONALS FROM HR PROFESSIONALS

1. Diversity and inclusion professionals are ambulance chasers. They search for conflict, so that is what they find. They don't try to reduce conflict, they blow it up. They sometimes manufacture unnecessary conflict. HR feels this way because D&I typically approaches them with issues involving conflict; however, because HR has tokenized the work of D&I, they approach HR aggressively to get them to do something about a matter that should have been focused on long ago.

2. Diversity and inclusion professionals are too one-dimensional. Every time D&I professionals show up, they only discuss gay issues, race issues, gender issues, disability issues, and so on. HR wants to know if D&I employees always have to make everything about these topics. Of course, it's not "always about race," but, there's some truth to this criticism. The problem is that D&I is normally only invited to the table to provide the minority perspective. When people don't want to hear about minority issues, they don't invite D&I professionals to the table.

3. Diversity and inclusion professionals try too hard to get in HR's business. Recruitment data is in HR's shop. Affirmative Action data is typically in HR's shop. Employee relations is in HR's shop. Labor relations is in HR's shop. Trainings are in HR's shop. Compensation and benefits and all the data associated with these functions are in HR's shop. Many HR professionals feel that D&I needs to find some business of their own! This is shortsighted and small-minded us-versus-them thinking because it's the company's data. However, if D&I is rude about securing the data or if they try to use the data in an effort to attack HR, naturally there will be conflict.

4. Diversity and inclusion doesn't focus on issues relevant to dominate culture matters. This means majority employees will only engage the D&I department when there is racial tension, when there's a need for cultural competency training, or when the company needs an equity presenter. They treat D&I like an invitation-only appendage of the company. If it's not about underrepresented communities, D&I need not attend. This is a major and pervasive problem.

5. The only requirement for being a D&I practitioner is being a member of a historically marginalized or underrepresented community. It's not a real disci-

pline. The truth is many D&I practitioners go into the work because they are a members of an under-represented group and they intimately understand how it feels to be treated unfairly. D&I also tends to be very interdisciplinary-people pursue it from a variety of professional backgrounds. It's also a younger discipline without many ways to formally learn how to become a practitioner. Also, compa-nies have in many ways tokenized the functional purpose of D&I, which fuels this feeling.

Diversity and inclusion and HR are both to blame for many of the previously listed criticisms. D&I can be quite one-dimensional, but that's because they've been mar-ginalized as an ancillary exercise of goodwill. Executives will also stick a D&I department in the company with no clue what they actually want them to accomplish. Many other departments will have specific goals with metrics and benchmarks included; D&I departments often do not. The D&I goals will include directives, for example, like creating a specified number of policies, conducting a certain number of trainings, or engage with a certain number of employees. These directives rarely lead to cultural shifts or changes. When D&I departments are created, they often do little to ensure there's a marked increase in the satisfaction of underrepresented employ-ees. Staff is not allowed to evaluate underrepresented employees in conjunction with HR on best practices that will lead to increases in overall employee satisfaction.

This brings me full circle to my initial theory. If HR and D&I professionals united, workplace equity and inclusion in organizations could be realized. Fighting only helps reinforce the workplace cultural challenges that led to the development of D&I departments to begin with. The juxtaposition between D&I and HR is palpable! D&I is usually very Brown and HR is usually very White. D&I is seen as progressive while HR is often seen as behind the times. D&I is seen as being an ally of the people, and HR is seen as the policing arm of the "man."

What if we merged? What if we expected HR professionals to come with D&I experience? What if we ensured there was an equity component to every function of HR? In my perfect world, HR's learning and organizational development would have equity and inclusion responsibilities hardwired into their work. Human resources directors would hire people with D&I expertise into roles on their teams. Recruitment would have diversity metrics and goals woven into every aspect of the work and we would hire people with proven success at hiring minorities into homogeneous work environments. In order for labor and employee relations professionals to be hired, they'd need to prove they are culturally competent and understand how supremacist ideology manifests in the workplace. Compensation and benefits professionals would be expected to be well-versed in market rates and wage disparities and would know how to respect-fully push against managers to avoid perpetuating earning gaps. What if we merged the two? What if we forced HR to be more inclusive? What if we made D&I more than a "good-to-go" entity by embedding it in the culture creation machine of companies known as HR?

In a perfect world, HR and D&I should unite to bring about systemic change. In the real world, however, we still have a long way to go.

CHAPTER 10

SUSTAINING A DIVERSE WORKFORCE

Building and sustaining a diverse workforce ain't easy; especially in less diverse parts of the country and particularly in some professional disciplines dominated by men. As you work through the challenges associated with diversifying your workforce, the potential issues may seem insurmountable at times. But, trust me, they are not. You can successfully build and maintain a diverse workforce. That effort does require leaders to champion the initiative, to be thoughtful, introspective, vulnerable at times, collaborative, open-minded, transparent, patient, consistent, and persistent. I don't use these words lightly. These are powerful leadership traits that will positively impact a workplace, its processes, and individual employee's lives.

This book showcases the challenges and opportunities of leading a diversity initiative and positively impacting your workplace. For those new to this work, learn from this book and the missteps of others so you can avoid similar pitfalls. For those who have tried to tackle a diversity initiative and run into similar challenges highlighted in this book, I want you to feel empowered with new tools to stay the course and keep trying.

In closing, I'd like to share with you a final case study that shows that this process can be successful.

Case Study: Never Saw a Person of Color
Jonathan, *CEO/Investment Firm*

OVERVIEW

Jonathan, the CEO of a small, successful Midwestern investment firm, decided after deep soul searching that he wanted to do a better job of connecting with more diverse communities. He wanted to make a shift from running an exclusively White, able-bodied, male team to having women, people of color, and age-diverse employees.. There were many days when Jonathan never saw a single person of color and didn't speak to women other than his wife. He felt as though he went straight to an exclusive "boys only" tree house in the morning then back home again.

DOING THE GOOD WORK

Soul searching was a revealing and difficult process for Jonathan, but he wanted to better understand why he was interested in pursuing this initiative. He hired a diversity consultant to help him discover those motivations and interests and to help him create a plan to build a more diverse workforce. Jonathan admitted that White guilt and charity fueled his motivations. He emphasized that wanting to diversify still had to co-exist with his desire to expand his company and amass more wealth for his employees, family, and clients. White guilt or not, there's nothing wrong with that!

THE PROCESS

Jonathan walked his entire executive team through the stages of this book. The consultant was put in charge of finding more diverse talent. Jonathan did everything right, including facing conflicts and challenges head-on to ultimately create a culture and environment of success for all employees.

SUMMARY

Fast-forward five years. Jonathan's firm is one of the most diverse wealth management firms in the Midwest and he's doubled the size of his company with a vastly diverse client base and staff. Jonathan has low turnover at his company and his employees are generally happy working at his firm. He has since built an internship program that is very diverse, which acts as a talent bench for his firm.

How did he accomplish his goal? To start with, he was very patient. He did not attempt to rush the process. It took Jonathan five years to move his initiatives forward.

He included his executive team from the start. There were multiple meetings over many weeks before anyone else in the organization new about the initiatives. The executive team supported his vision and helped keep the process moving forward once it started. While some liked the "club" atmosphere, they all agreed that diversity could bring new approaches and new ideas to the company. This would ultimately also help attract new clients.

Jonathan rolled out a recruitment strategy based on current vacancies and informed placement of new, underrepresented employees in new roles. He held his hiring managers responsible for ensuring that their workforce was more diverse.

Jonathan hired local talent, which made connecting them to the local community a nonissue. He changed the evaluation structure of his agency, establishing a 360-degree evaluation structure. He surveyed his workforce twice yearly to keep his finger on the pulse of his workplace environment and culture.

Jonathan also celebrated the communication and interpersonal diversity of his new workforce. He wanted them to be exactly who they were because his clients connected with authenticity and professionalism. The variety of styles within his workforce helped him expand his client base and better fit individual client personalities.

Every leader can have the same success Jonathan did; the recipe is in the pages of this book. You can create a better workplace, a better workforce, and you can reap the rewards a diverse and inclusive work environment brings.

FINAL THOUGHTS

The first part of my career was spent in HR. I helped dominant culture executives understand why having a homogeneous workforce in the 21st century was short-sighted and a liability to their companies. Today most executives and leaders now understand that in a global marketplace they must have a workforce that's nimble and diverse. Many still struggle to accomplish and/or sustain their diversity initiatives.

FOR MORE RESOURCES GO TO:
WORKPLACECHANGES.COM

37762609R00073

Made in the USA
San Bernardino, CA
03 June 2019